T0275686

Securing Social Media in the Enterprise

Securing Social Media in the Enterprise

Henry Dalziel

Contributing Editor
Nicholas Arvanitis

AMSTERDAM • BOSTON • HEIDELBERG • LONDON
NEW YORK • OXFORD • PARIS • SAN DIEGO
SAN FRANCISCO • SINGAPORE • SYDNEY • TOKYO
Syngress is an imprint of Elsevier

ELSEVIER

SYNGRESS.

Syngress is an imprint of Elsevier
225 Wyman Street, Waltham, MA 02451, USA

Notices
Knowledge and best practice in this field are constantly changing. As new research and
experience broaden our understanding, changes in research methods or professional
practices, may become necessary.

Practitioners and researchers must always rely on their own experience and knowledge in
evaluating and using any information or methods described herein. In using such information
or methods they should be mindful of their own safety and the safety of others, including
parties for whom they have a professional responsibility.

To the fullest extent of the law, neither the Publisher nor the authors, contributors, or editors,
assume any liability for any injury and/or damage to persons or property as a matter of products
liability, negligence or otherwise, or from any use or operation of any methods, products,
instructions, or ideas contained in the material herein.

ISBN: 978-0-12-804180-2

British Library Cataloguing-in-Publication Data
A catalogue record for this book is available from the British Library

Library of Congress Cataloging-in-Publication Data
A catalog record for this book is available from the Library of Congress

For Information on all Syngress publications
visit our website at http://store.elsevier.com/

CONTENTS

AUTHOR BIOGRAPHY

Henry Dalziel is a serial education entrepreneur, founder of Concise Ac Ltd, online cybersecurity blogger and e-book author. He writes for the Concise-Courses.com blog and has developed numerous cybersecurity continuing education courses and books. Concise Ac Ltd develops and distributes continuing education content [books and courses] for cybersecurity professionals seeking skill enhancement and career advancement. The company was recently accepted onto the UK Trade & Investment's (UKTI) Global Entrepreneur Programme (GEP).

CONTRIBUTING EDITOR BIOGRAPHY

Nicholas Arvanitis is a Security Engineer at a startup in New York City. Prior to that he was a key member of the security team at one of the largest worldwide exchanges, where he was responsible for protecting critical market infrastructure and software. Nicholas spent over a decade before that as a penetration tester and security consultant, building and breaking systems and applications, and passionately teaching others how to do so across the globe at conferences such as Black Hat and Defcon.

CHAPTER 1

Introduction

This book starts with a review of where the skills you'll learn about are most applicable, and the relevance in today's security industry, both for offensive and defensive security professionals. Then, it digs into some techniques and methodologies to assess social media risk and, of course, some counter measures.

Disclaimer: Some of these concepts are a little difficult to understand without a real world example to relate to. So we use a lot of practical examples. For all the examples in here, including the images, we have added their original links. In other words, everything is open source and public. There are a few cases where we've used somebody's details and had to obscure certain things. However, we've only obscured open source screenshots, so it's all material anybody could collect.

Social media has received a lot of focus: namely, how you control it and restrict what your users can do? Why? Because social media plays a key part in many attackers' methodologies. In fact, a lot of reconnaissance work revolves around the use of social media. If we look at what's happened over the last few years, social media has been the catalyst for rich targeting capabilities that lead to a growing number of security compromises and, data "leaks."

Interestingly, some of these "leaks" have been well documented and include Target, Sony Records, and JP Morgan Chase. One of the key factors in many targeted compromises is that they started with some form of spear phishing to deliver the initial exploit.

If we take a step back, many of the compromises use personal information in one way or another. One of the primary attack objectives, especially against retailers, is acquisition of personal information and credit card data; it's a relatively easy attack vector with straightforward ways to monetize the data. Attackers will often target organizational web applications, as these applications contain business logic and have legitimate access to backend data stores housing this sensitive data. This explains the popularity of attacks targeting web applications such as SQL injection.

Another major vector that played a key role in the Target attack was compromising the chain of trust. The Target breach was the result of a breach of one of Target's providers. They maintained Target's air conditioning units, and the network access they had into Target's environment was used as an entry point.

Spear Phishing

2011

2014

ICANN Targeted in Spear Phishing Attack | Enhanced Security Measures Implemented

This page is available in: العربية | 中文 | Português | Русский | Español | Français | English

in f ✈ ⊚ ⊠ +

ICANN is investigating a recent intrusion into our systems. We believe a 'spear phishing' attack was initiated in late November 2014. It involved email messages that were crafted to appear to come from our own domain being sent to members of our staff. The attack resulted in the compromise of the email credentials of several ICANN staff members.

One of the biggest attack vectors on everyone's mind is spear phishing. This is a screenshot of the spear phishing email sent to RSA before it was breached in 2011. That initial email was crafted and contained a spreadsheet with an embedded exploit for Flash that was the initial foothold compromise of the targeted users' machines, and was the starting point for the attack.

This screenshot from The Internet Corporation for Assigned Names and Numbers (ICANN) in late December 2014 shows ICANN investigating a recent intrusion into their system. It's thus clear that the same attack vectors that were popular in 2011 and before are just as relevant today.

Phishing is definitely an active vector, and one that many organizations are familiar with. The reason we bring it up is because we need to craft an effective strategy to counter the impact of spear phishing. So, for context's sake, spear phishing is a focused and well-crafted phishing attack on a specific target.

In order for the spear phish to be successful, you need to craft a message your target will almost certainly open and act on. The message itself could contain an attachment, a link, or something similar. In order to craft such a message—that is, personalized and believable—a lot of knowledge about your intended target is required. You probably guessed that social media is one of the many channels to get this information. And we'll talk a little more about that in a while.

Robin Sage

Robin Sage is a fictional American cyber threat analyst. She was created in December 2009 by Thomas Ryan, a security specialist and White hat hacker from New York. Thomas Ryan later became infamous after he self-anointed himself to be an undercover snitch for the FBI during the Occupy Wall Street Movement by using a fake identity to make friends with others in the movement and then forwarding email lists he acquired. Ryan outed himself accidentally by sending the email lists to the media with public reaction universally condemning him as a clown.[1] Her name was taken from a training exercise of United States Army Special Forces.[2]

"Robin Sage" as she appeared on social networking pages.

To add even more context, it's important to mention research conducted by security researcher Tom Ryan, in 2009. He essentially created a fake persona for a fictional threat analyst called Robin Sage. He managed to establish a vast network of connections for this persona, including representatives of the Information Security, Defense and Intelligence Communities. He presented this research at BlackHat, and highlighted how many of the connections with these people were enabled by social media. His research showed that you could engage in various circles and build credibility for someone that's not real, even in circles where there should be a much greater awareness of security. That's an interesting perspective because we're in the age of sharing, where knowledge is shared incredibly easily and very rapidly.

Regardless of the site you use, social media is huge, and people are increasingly posting more of their activities, both professional and personal, online for the world to see. To make matters worse, most people don't know about or don't understand the value in many of the security and privacy settings available to them.

People are tangentially aware of some of the dangers and risks involved. When asked, one of the common rebuttals is "My information is private. So, if I don't connect with you, you can't view what I'm putting up there." That initial connection is really what most people rely on for security. In this case, Tom was able to create this persona and actually get this person to connect with many people across different industry sectors. As highlighted before, this includes defense, intelligence, and computer security professionals.

So arguably, he was able to connect with people who were supposed to be more technically savvy and aware of these types of threats. We recommend you look at his research, because it's really interesting. Essentially, the character he created was even getting job offers. What's really interesting is how far this can go and how effective this can be.

If the people who know more about technology and are more aware of threats are vulnerable to these types of deceptions and attacks, what would happen to regular people? If you are targeting an organization with people who are not as tech or security savvy, they are likely to be more vulnerable.

We want to delve into targeted attacks a little more because as enterprises, those are the concerns that we really should be worried about. Again, we're going to talk about targeted attacks, and then relate it back to where social media plays a role.

Our definition of a targeted attack is when an attacker is specifically aiming to compromise your organization with a clear goal. Another example of such an attack is the recent attack on Sony.

The attackers had a very specific objective and they explicitly targeted Sony. They achieved an outcome that was their ultimate goal for the compromise.

It's not like they had a single exploit that they were opportunistically compromising multiple organizations with. They weren't necessarily trying to phish just anyone on the internet. They were specifically targeting Sony, and as an enterprise, these attacks should concern everyone, as they are indicative of a motivated and focused adversary.

CHAPTER 2

Cyber Kill Chain

Cyber Kill Chain

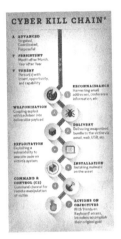

http://www.lockheedmartin.com/us/
what-we-do/information-technology/
cyber-security/cyber-kill-chain.html

Researchers at Lockheed Martin created a model of a typical framework for how to think about targeted attacks. They created a model called the Cyber Kill Chain. The Kill Chain really represents a sequence of actions that an attacker will go through to achieve their ultimate objectives. They've laid it out really nicely and we've linked the paper from Lockheed so you can read it when you have the time. However, at a higher level, there are a number of steps involved in the Kill Chain.

1. Start out with reconnaissance
2. Weaponization
3. Delivery
4. Exploitation
5. Installation
6. Establishing Command and Control
7. Achieve Your Ultimate Actions and Objectives

The one we want to focus on for this book is reconnaissance. As you see on the slide, reconnaissance is not only about harvesting information such as email addresses and conference information. The role of reconnaissance is to find out as much about your target as possible. That's the first step of an attacker's kill chain.

When we talk about reconnaissance, it's almost exactly what the term implies. As an attacker, if you consider targeting an organization by breaking into their systems, applications, or computers over the internet, you want to perform quite a bit of reconnaissance to find out what they have exposed on the internet.

We don't mean to pick specifically on Sony, but they're an example that's still fresh in the public's mind. If you think about Sony as an abstract target or real-world entity, when aiming to compromise the corporation as a computer-based attacker you need specific things to aim at. You need an idea of what services are running on their machines. As such, you want at the very least a list of active IP addresses associated with Sony to identify these machines.

Once you have a goal, or specific target in mind, you need to acquire more information during your reconnaissance. You need to identify what software is running on those services and their versions. This will help you enumerate vulnerabilities so that you can start to craft and weaponize exploits for these services.

In the same way that you perform reconnaissance on networks or systems, an attacker targeting an organization through its employees needs to perform reconnaissance on who those employees are.

From an attacker's perspective, you need to know who the key people associated with an organization are, and what kind of information you can get from them. Ask yourself a few questions:

✓ Can you find out email addresses?
✓ Can you find out personal information?
✓ Can you start to link those people to their social networks and start to find out more information about them?

The more time and work you put into reconnaissance, the more likely you will succeed in achieving your ultimate objectives. In other words, the more time and effort you put into reconnaissance and getting a really solid profile of your target, the higher your chance of success. It's the law of large numbers, right? If we throw a stone into a room with two people in it, we're less likely to hit someone than if we throw a stone into a room with a hundred people. With this example in mind, the more data and facts you have, the better equipped you are to be able to compromise your target. Reconnaissance is really important from an attacker's perspective.

Another point that is important to understand is the attack surface the organization has exposed. If we look at techniques used to compromise organizations in the past, and we touched on it before, there were attack vectors that target the infrastructure. In other words, attackers used to target operating systems. With so many remote exploits, it wasn't hard to see why.

These days, you don't see that anymore. Security has improved dramatically and rapidly. Compared to before, not as many services are exposed on the internet. Those that are, you can guarantee are hardened and well monitored.

Attackers began to move toward web-based applications, but most large organizations are savvy about this and have started to understand that vulnerabilities such as SQL injection can be pretty critical. That's why they started building more defenses and monitoring around web applications.

Attackers have pivoted once again, and are looking for an easier and broader attack surface. What better attack surface than an organization's employees?

Let's consider just the asymmetry of these two attack vectors. When an attacker is targeting an organization's internet-facing infrastructure, chances are good you're going to have really savvy systems administrators monitoring that infrastructure. Compare this to an employee who has been in an organization for 60 years and is just starting to get comfortable with email and similar technologies.

It's really easy to see which aspect of an organization is more likely to be attacked. This asymmetry plays a big role in any attack because the attack surface of employees itself is huge.

Attack Surface

Citigroup

Market Cap **$145.14 B**
As of May 2014

+ **Follow** (111)

At a Glance		Forbes Lists	
Industry: **Major Banks**		**#98** World's Most	
Founded: **1812**		Valuable Brands	
Country: **United States**		**#16** Global 2000	
CEO: **Michael Corbat**		**#70** in Sales	
Website: www.citigroup.com		**#31** in Profit	
Employees: **251,000**		**#15** in Assets	
Sales: **$94.06 B**		**#38** in Market value	
Headquarters: **New York, New York**			

http://funny-pics-fun.com/wp-content/
uploads/Funny-Employee-At-Work-Is-All-
The-Fun-11.jpg

http://www.forbes.com/companies/citigroup/

We pulled a slide from the Forbes site on Citigroup and saw that they have 251,000 employees. As an attacker, if we want to target Citigroup, why would we try to take down their front door and all their associated services and servers, which are likely highly monitored? Why would we do that when we could potentially target any of those 251,000 employees who we can find information on and probably have a higher likelihood of success?

The question here really becomes "how do I gather information on those employees so I can start crafting those attacks we spoke about before, such as spear phishing?" We're going to dig into a methodology for that.

One last point we want to talk about is the old mechanisms of compromising an organization by attacking an application or server. Once you've compromised the application or server, you're pretty liable to have a foothold on the network somewhere. However, you're probably within a restricted network segment like a DMZ or potentially a subnetwork, with some related services.

You're still going to have to work on compromising other systems to or gain access to other data. There are still a lot of steps required for an attacker to follow and chances are good there's a lot of monitoring in place on those network segments.

If you start doing things on the network, there's likely to be some sort of IDS, IPS, or web application firewalls or other filtering devices. If we are an attacker, we need to turn such things on their head and compromise an employee of an organization. By the nature of the work that they are required to do, such an employee has access to certain systems and data; they're already on the internal network.

Many organizations are starting to get network segmentation right, but a lot of organizations still aren't there. The payout for the attacker targeting an employee is incredibly high, and that's why a lot of attacks have shifted this way, to this vector.

With that context out of the way, we want to delve a little more into open source intelligence. It's a really broad topic and its roots are in the gathering of actual intelligence, such as the activity conducted by many nation states. If you think about the intelligence community, they have multiple sources of intelligence. These include human, signal, and open source intelligence.

We consider OSINT specifically in the context of an attacker who wants to gather information on a target organization. The key here is it's open source, so you're harvesting information from sources like the web, social media, and other openly accessible information sources. This makes it very valuable, because you generally don't leave too much of a footprint.

Again, the topic is huge and it can be fairly difficult to understand because there's less science and a lot more art in it. Gathering this sort of open source intelligence when you are targeting an organization is an art form. It's thus important to have some sort of methodology to base and guide your work and efforts on.

In terms of methodology, we're going to dig a little deeper in the following sections. We're going to dive into how you perform each step. At a higher level, you go through a number of specific steps in building a profile on a target organization and specific individuals within that organization. That methodology starts with establishing a baseline form of identity.

Remember, we're talking about taking a real world individual and understanding what links them to their digital presence. If you want to think about that in a practical example, we like to use email addresses for that. One person could have multiple email addresses, but each email address is unique and uniquely tied to a single person in most cases.

The other interesting thing about email addresses is they are used as identifiers or "logins" to specific applications, including many social media accounts. Further down the line, email addresses are also a fallback for certain events. For example, if you want to reset somebody's password using many applications' password recovery mechanisms, having an email address is essential.

Methodology

1. Baseline Identity
2. Link Analysis
3. Investigation
4. Correlation
5. Profiling

You want to first establish a baseline identity and then take the next step to start to analyze where that identity is linked. If we have established an email address for somebody, we want to know where they are using that email address. Is that email address used to login to Facebook? If we have an idea of somebody's digital identity, do they have a LinkedIn to go with that? Do they have a Twitter account? Do they have an Instagram account? Is somebody using a specific handle or username across multiple social media accounts? Or is it a derivative of their name or an email address?

You want to try to establish the links between multiple media channels and the identity you are targeting. This matters across an organization. In other words, if I am targeting a specific organization, what are the links to its employees? What are the links to other organizations? We'll dig more into this in a while. However, to help build the background, we want to discuss these high-level steps first.

Step 3 is an interesting one, because that's where a lot of creativity comes into play. When you are doing the work we mentioned, it's a lot less science and a lot more art, but it takes a little bit of investigation and open mindedness. This is because it's the time you get creative and become a detective, spy, and data analyst, all at once.

What you really want to do is work through a process where you are taking a little bit of information in the form of a baseline identity, expanding that to as much data as you can through link analysis, and then investigating each lead.

In the investigation phase, what you're really doing is coming up with a hypothesis and then trying to prove it. For example, if we find that a specific individual we're targeting has a LinkedIn and Twitter account, we want to look for other media as well.

Does that person have a Facebook account that shares something in common with the other accounts? Whether it is an email address, a profile photo, an affiliation, or anything similar, we want it. We want to go through these deductive steps and investigate aspects such as relationships between people. We'll ask ourselves, are these two people that work for this target organization linked in other ways? Do they have similar hobbies or similar interests?

You tend to go through a lot of investigative steps and, at this stage, you might discredit certain links you discovered or increase the likelihood of validity of others. You might even enumerate different identities you didn't come across for that specific person and then cycle through the process again. That phase is a lot of work; a lot of detective work.

In the fourth phase, you want to correlate all the information you've found. Again, it's taking a lot of data, and bringing it down to more of a core element. You could say something like:

"In my target organization, these are all the people I can find information on that are associated with this organization. For this specific individual, this is all the information I have. This is what social media channels they are active on and this is the information they are giving out."

Then you want to start building a profile in the final phase to use for effective targeting. Again, that's on a macro organizational scale. On the micro scale, it's for each specific individual.

Just to recap the methodology:

1. You start by establishing a baseline identity
2. You analyze the links and other potential identities
3. You do a lot of detective work to gain the information you need
4. You correlate what you have and you build a profile (We'll dig into that shortly)

Establishing a baseline identity is interesting. We touched on the fact that email addresses are a good jump-off point because they often link accounts and emails are generally a fairly cheap commodity. There are many ways to get somebody's email address. One is to dig through conferences and collect business cards from people. Another great one is to reach out to business development or employees in sales-related roles, as they're more eager to grow their networks and share contact information.

You can also just use search engines to find them. Many tools can do this, but we use a common open source tool called The Harvester. We dump in a target organization such as Hubspot; their domain is hubspot.com. The Harvester goes out and finds many email addresses that are associated with Hubspot as a domain.

If you take a look through those quickly, you can see there are some generic ones like info@hubspot.com, hubspotgermany@hubspot.com, and success@hubspot.com. These are ones you should consider as not really useful as they don't associate with specific individuals. But in between them, there are a host of valid email addresses for people, such as mjacobson@hubspot.com, pcaputo, dshaw, and bsingleton; these are all likely real people.

From this, you already understand it's a cheap tool. We ran it and it found this data for us. It was collected from the web, so we're not leaving any footprints at Hubspot. It's not like we're port scanning an organization that could make them aware that we're doing something. We're just collecting information openly. With this information, we can do a lot of other things.

From here, we can take these email addresses and start looking for associations on social media, and more. We haven't identified anyone's identity at the moment. The other thing we take away from this is it gives us an idea of the network's naming convention for email addresses.

Remember, we ultimately want to deliver targeted spear phishing emails to people, so email addresses are a great target because they give us a mechanism by which to deliver our attack. We can see that Hubspot's naming convention looks like it might be the first initial of the person's first name and then their last name @Hubspot.com.

When you look at jparker or mfitzgerald, you know these addresses are useful because if we find other employees, maybe via Twitter or LinkedIn or something like that, we can probably reverse engineer their email address out of it. We generally tend to work off email addresses as a starting point, because ultimately that's our desired endpoint.

There are many tools that are pretty interesting because they automate a lot of this. While we'll talk about automation a little later, right now it's important to understand how this works manually because when you're using these tools, you know what value they add, what their limitations are, and how they work under the hood because you know how to do things manually.

Another way to really find a lot of information on people is by visiting the target organization's webpage. If we were an attacker targeting Lockheed Martin as an organization, we could visit their webpage. Every organization has a page that has an "About Us" section and, in many cases, it has details on the leadership team or their executives, which are the high value targets in an organization.

We've literally taken this screenshot off their website and have placed the link at the bottom of the slide. But if we take a quick snapshot of this information, this is Lockheed Martin's Chief Executive Officer and there's a wealth of information offered to me by their very own website.

CHAPTER 3

Baseline Identity

Baseline Identity

Marillyn A. Hewson

**Chairman, President and Chief Executive Officer
Lockheed Martin Corporation**

Marillyn A. Hewson is Chairman, President and Chief Executive Officer of Lockheed Martin Corporation. She previously held a variety of increasingly responsible executive positions with the Corporation, including President and Chief Operating Officer and Executive Vice President of Lockheed Martin's Electronic Systems business area.

In her 31 years with Lockheed Martin, Ms. Hewson has held several operational leadership positions including President of Lockheed Martin Systems Integration; Executive Vice President of Global Sustainment for Lockheed Martin Aeronautics; President and General Manager of Kelly Aviation Center, L.P., an affiliate of Lockheed Martin; and President of Lockheed Martin Logistics Services. She has also served in key corporate executive roles, including Senior Vice President of Corporate Shared Services; Vice President of Global Supply Chain Management; and Vice President of Corporate Internal Audit.

Ms. Hewson serves on the Board of Directors of DuPont and previously chaired the Sandia Corporation Board of Directors from 2010 to 2013. She served on the Board of Directors of Carpenter Technology Corporation from 2002 through 2006. In September 2013, Ms. Hewson was appointed by President Barack Obama to the President's Export Council, the principal national advisory committee on international trade. She is Vice Chairman-elect of the Aerospace Industries Association, and is an Associate Fellow of the American

High Res Photo
Download a PDF Version
Follow Marillyn on LinkedIn

[+] Emails found:
----
info@hubspot.com
111111@forward.hubspot.com
mjacobson@hubspot.com
hubspotgermany@hubspot.com
@hubspot.com
pcaputa@hubspot.com
dshah@hubspot.com
careers@hubspot.com
success@hubspot.com
bsingleton@hubspot.com
marketing@hubspot.com
dfernandez@hubspot.com
privacy@hubspot.com
jstehler@hubspot.com
tpetr@hubspot.com
ci@hubspot.com
trundell@hubspot.com
gchomatas@hubspot.com
pgandhi@hubspot.com
jhaber@hubspot.com
mfitzgerald@hubspot.com
jparker@hubspot.com

http://www.lockheedmartin.com/us/who-we-are/leadership/hewson.html

We get her full name, Marillyn A. Hewson and an idea of what her history within the organization is. She's been there for 31 years and then a little further down, it talks about other associations that she is connected with.

She's on the board of directors of Dupont, previously chaired the Sandia Corporation board of directors, and has been associated with Carpenter Technology Corporation. All of these links are really useful for us, because we can start to understand the context and understand she might have a professional network that links with Sandia, Dupont, and others.

As an attacker, we can try to target these other organizations too because they may be useful avenues into our ultimate target, and we can look at the organization and its employees and the links between these people.

Going back to the website, it offers us a high-resolution photo of this lady and also gives us a link to Marillyn's LinkedIn. There are other additional links and information I can follow, but it's definitely a useful first step.

Doing this kind of work is effective because you're not leaving a footprint. Again, we are accessing their website just like anybody else would. You can take this further because there are many sources for finding information on specific organizations.

If you look at conference presentations on Slideshare, you can sometimes see people talking about various topics, and you can link them with their source organization. For listed companies, you can pull their filings with the Securities Exchange Commission in the United States—a listed company has to give filings and they'll list their executives in these filings. What we're trying to tell you is there are many ways to find information about key employees within an organization. That's a good initial point attackers start from.

If it hasn't already been obvious, social media really is a goldmine for an attacker and this is because we can find a lot of context on a target using social media channels. Professionally, we can start to understand their history, where they went to school, their areas of interest, key people they're associated with and their professional network.

We can start to gain a better understanding of people's hobbies, interests, topics that are near and dear to them, and their personal associations—the possibilities are limitless.

You need to take a step back and appreciate the ultimate goal, and understand that for an attacker, the more context they have, the better equipped they are to deliver a successful exploit, and that becomes increasingly valuable.

For example, think about two scenarios. I'm an attacker targeting a specific individual and I have no context on them, other than perhaps their name and their email address. What's my best bet? I could pick a topic, send them a spear phishing email to maybe say "Hey, here's a catalog of information on my organization. Please open it." They are more likely to ignore that.

If we have rich context and we can understand that our target is potentially a runner, we have run some similar races, we have other hobbies or interests in common, I've seen some pictures on social media, I know she takes her dog along with her on runs, and I'm a dog lover, I can potentially befriend her with a fake profile.

On social media, we can really send a very well-crafted email along the lines of "You know I've created a blog. I'm tracking all of my run statistics. I'm posting pictures of me and my dog running" and then I put a link in the message. She's more likely to click that and my chances of success are higher. Social media is valuable from that perspective, because it really helps us get more into a target's psyche and thinking.

Some very useful elements we can get from social media are things like geolocation. Many attacks are effective from close proximity. The context of this is targeted attacks, and for targeted attacks and red teaming, it's important to think out of the box.

Geolocation

As such, a traditional penetration tester would look at a specific set of services on the internet and would scan them before trying to compromise them. For real-world attackers, there are no real boundaries. For one with enough motivation, it's very likely that a legitimate tactic is to go to your key employees' homes and try to compromise their home wireless network. In fact, you can even try to break into their homes and, under certain circumstances, access their system physically.

These elements are important, but other things start to become interesting there too because if we can understand somebody's habits, and we see that every Sunday morning our target spends time in a specific Starbucks reading the news and tweeting from there, we have an open book. We could go to that Starbucks and try to set up a fake access point to Man-in-the-Middle them and gain access to some of their data.

Geolocation is really valuable for many reasons. Think about the context of how social media is really used. Most people are posting and creating content on social media from their mobile devices. Perhaps on a corporate machine, location services are disabled, but on mobile devices, location services often are enabled.

When they are tweeting, posting to Instagram, or even if they check-in on Facebook or Foursquare, I can start to understand their movements. In this specific case, we took a tweet from a gentleman who tweeted something about the Super Bowl on the 2nd of February last year. In case you don't remember, it was Super Bowl Sunday, and the time of this tweet was 7:13 in the morning.

Chances are that somebody's tweeting that from home at that time, right? And he geotagged it. So, by clicking on that pin on Twitter, it will give you a set of coordinates. You can dump those coordinates straight into Google Maps and it plots it on a map for you.

In this case, this person we were targeting worked for Hubspot. So, we can start to map out how far they are from work and start to understand what their habits are. You can take that further and dig on Google Maps Street View and get a good idea of their neighborhood if you are going to go case the joint.

Many other attacks are valuable from a certain geographic and proximity perspective. Geolocation is fantastic to extract from social media and that's really valuable for understanding the physical patterns of a potential target.

One of the other hand, amazing thing that social media offers is network analysis. It helps us understand a specific individual's network, who they are associated with and what topics they are interested in. We do this because it helps us craft an attack and get into what that person is potentially open to, who they connect with, and what topics and industries they are interested in.

CHAPTER 4

Network Analysis

Network Analysis

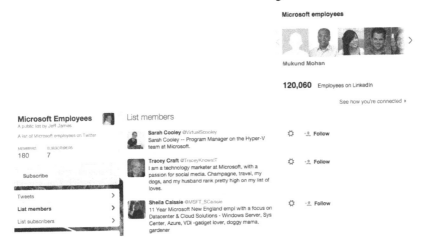

Network analysis is also interesting when targeting a specific organization. For example, if we wanted to target Microsoft as an organization, it's really easy for us to find a lot of information on Microsoft's employees.

On the top right of the slide, we took a screenshot from LinkedIn and all we did was search for Microsoft as an employer. It tells us about over 120,000 employees work for Microsoft and lists them on LinkedIn, which is a fantastic starting point. That is a target-rich environment, because some of them have pictures and we could start to do more research based on them.

We also searched on Twitter for Microsoft employees and a number of lists of people were created on Twitter with Microsoft's employees; here's an example of a list created by Jeff James. He's called it a "list of Microsoft employees that he knows are on Twitter."

There are 180 members, so it's a rich environment for us to start with, and gives us a lot of information. We get a photograph and a full name as well as a number of other details. We found:

- Sara Cooley, a program manager on the Hyper-V team at Microsoft.
- Tracey Craft, she's in Technology Marketing at Microsoft. She loves social media and we already start to learn lots of her other interests. She loves champagne, traveling, big dogs, and her husband ranks pretty high on her list of loves. As an attacker, that gives us a lot of context.
- Sheila Caissie, who has been at Microsoft for 11 years, is based in New England and focused on data center and cloud solutions. She loves gadgets, dogs, and gardening.

This stuff is really valuable, because from here, we can start to mine each of their networks. We could follow Sara and start to understand what topics she is interested in, what she's tweeting about and then figure out who's following Sara and possibly enumerate more Microsoft employees or business partners that way.

On the flipside, we could look into whom Sara is following and use that as a channel. Then, we could correlate this information against other social networks. Sara's handle is virtualscoolie. Could I take that and look for it on Instagram? Could I look for that on Facebook? Could I look for that on Pinterest?

I can really start to chop and change this data and you will see that from a little bit of work, the scope of the data really gets big again for a potential attacker.

Analyzing people's networks is incredibly valuable and really useful because it helps you gain a solid handle on common connections. Think about it for a second. Connecting with somebody on LinkedIn is sometimes a gamble because as an attacker, it's difficult to create a fake profile that's really believable.

Nevertheless it's a very effective tactic and certain nation states use it. I don't want to say they use it for APT, because it's an overblown term. But if you put it in that category, there are certain nation states that love it. In fact, they begin their attacks and campaigns by associating with target employees on LinkedIn, and work from there.

That network effect of social media is huge, because if you take a step back and look at your own use of social media, you're more liable to connect with somebody who wants to connect with you if they are also connected to your other connections right?

It starts to show social trust and actual social networks in the literal sense. For a lack of a better term, that "interconnectivity" is really key. It is something that is great for an attacker to exploit. As such, network analysis is very valuable as a starting point to build a massive set of data.

There are many lower tech attacks that are possible by social media, and that's one of the beauties of it as an attack channel. The technical bars are a lot lower. If you think about compromising an organization via a web application, you need to understand a lot about application security. For example, to conduct a successful SQL injection attack, you would need to know about how you would manipulate queries as well as exfiltrate the data, and this is technically complex.

The same issues exist for compromising a network server. You might need knowledge of exploitation, and be able to create zero-day exploits, where a lot of the social engineering attacks are low tech and mining social media really just takes being able to understand connections between people and personalities.

It's a really low technical bar for an attacker, which makes it fairly cheap. One of the massive wins that you can get out of something like social media is less obvious and it's in the form of competitive intelligence.

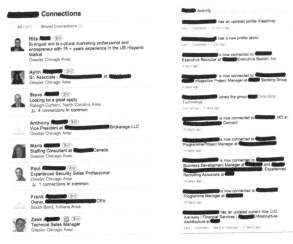

What we've done on this slide is taken screenshots that we've sanitized a little from one of our own connections on LinkedIn. This specific person is technically savvy and we were colleagues 10 years ago in the same organization. We've since been in a lot of different organizations respectively. We were both in the security consulting space, and what's interesting here is that this specific technically savvy person has a handle on security, but hasn't locked down the viewability of their connections on LinkedIn.

So, in many cases, where you should only be able to view shared connections, his entire professional network is wide open to us. As a consultant, that is pretty much gold. His address book and network are really where his business comes from.

Whether you're in accounting or law or management consulting or finance, it's the same in any professional field. Professional networking is critical and if we were in a competitive organization and viewing this data, we could potentially find customers that we could approach; we could find business partners. There's a lot of competitive intelligence for us there.

On that angle, if you look at monitoring this individual's activity on the right hand side, there's a wealth of information we could get there if we were in a competitive situation. If we take a look at some of the updates, he's connected to somebody at a specific organization, a project manager, and to recruiters.

That starts to get interesting, because we can start to establish a pattern of behavior here. If we went through these, 19 hours ago this person updated the headline on their profile. A day ago they added a profile photo. Three days ago they connected to an executive recruiter.

There are a few other recruiters they connected to recently. Maybe this person is potentially looking for another job. Maybe they're updating their LinkedIn profile, connecting with recruiters, or maybe they want to explore the market.

If we are in a competitive situation, we could potentially target that person and try to entice them away, or if we were more nefarious, we could potentially use this information to our advantage. We could potentially use it to alert their current employer, or use the threat of alerting their current employer to put pressure on this specific individual to give us something; old school blackmail.

The possibilities are pretty limitless. What the information gives us is a good angle, because this person likely is looking for a job and they are open to connecting with recruiters. Clearly, what we need to do is establish a fake profile as a recruiter. Again, it goes to that point that we spoke about earlier in the Robin Sage discussion, where people said their media was closed and details should only be available to those who are connected with them.

In getting to that initial point, people are very likely to connect with recruiters. Salespersons are very likely to connect with potential customers, and prospects. There's always an angle by which you could get somebody to connect with you. Understanding what they are interested in, and their behaviors are really key in that respect.

Another potentially low-tech angle is good old traditional blackmail. Whether it's an email address or the way they use a naming convention of the user name, people often link their disparate personas on the internet or have something in common. They often use the same handle for their username across multiple media. Although it takes a lot of digging, if you can find those linkages, you can potentially find their behavior and something to use against them.

Blackmail

For example, Ashley Madison's tagline is "Life Is Short. Have An Affair." If we find a target who has the same handle, or the same email address, and is registered on this specific site, we could potentially use that to blackmail that person within our target organization. Again, that's a very low-tech attack, but it is a very effective one.

We don't necessarily need to target people with very visible profiles like the CEO of an organization, or a CFO. We could use these types of attacks against people who will give us additional access. Maybe I want to gain physical access to an office, and we need to blackmail somebody who works at the front desk. They are more likely to look the other way if we have something on them.

It's really relevant in this case as well, where you start to understand what the threats posed by using an online identity in multiple places are and how they can be linked together to build a profile on you.

We've talked a lot about a very high level methodology and how to execute it, and we've gone into a few examples of how you can look at certain things. The topic is really huge.

We also want to talk a little bit about automation, because although it's possible to do all of this manually and it's definitely one of the best vectors when you're starting to learn these things, if you're doing this work on a regular basis, automating certain attacks is a great force multiplier. We want to look at some measures that will help with a little bit of heavy lifting.

Aggregators are really useful. Many aggregators like checkusernames. com and peekyou.com are great because you can punch in an alias, or a username, and check what social media networks that alias is available on. It is really useful for cases where people use the same handle or alias across multiple social networks.

CHAPTER 5

Aggregators

We've talked a lot about a very high level methodology and how to execute it, and we've gone into a few examples of how you can look at certain things. The topic is really huge.

We also want to talk a little bit about automation, because although it's possible to do all of this manually and it's definitely one of the best vectors when you're starting to learn these things, if you're doing this work on a regular basis, automating certain attacks is a great force multiplier. We want to look at some measures that will help with a little bit of heavy lifting.

Aggregators are really useful. Many aggregators like checkusernames.com and peekyou.com are great because you can punch in an alias, or a username, and check what social media networks that alias is available on. It is really useful for cases where people use the same handle or alias across multiple social networks.

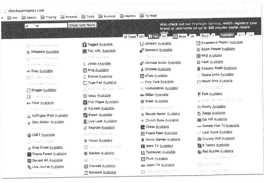

In this case, we found a target's handle via Twitter. We punched it into the site and immediately we can see that the same alias is being used on YouTube, LinkedIn, Tumblr, Pinterest, Imgur, Wordpress, Reddit, Vimeo, Yelp, Foursquare, and a couple of others. That gives us a great starting point.

We could go and find this information out manually of course. It would take more work, but for the three seconds it takes to punch it into the site, it saves a lot of time. If you're doing this manually for a large host of usernames, it could literally take days. Automation becomes a force multiplier. Tools like these are really valuable if you find an alias from somewhere—all you have to do is insert it into an aggregator, look and see where else it is.

If we went looking to impersonate this user, or attack some of their social network, we now know that we can probably register this account on Flickr or Blogger, where it's available, and start impersonating the user on those accounts or media. This makes aggregators really useful.

Another really interesting tool is Snoopy, developed by the guys at SensePost. Snoopy is helpful because it works with geolocation very well. At a high level, what Snoopy really does is listen for Wi-Fi beaconing from mobile devices. If you take a step back, you will notice that once your smartphone or tablet has connected to a wireless network or multiple wireless networks, the device constantly beacons via Wi-Fi searching for these known networks to associate to the access points.

SensePost Snoopy

Forget about the NSA, there's a new drone named Snoopy that can steal all your smartphone data while it's flying in the sky. A group of hackers created the drone and will show it off at Black Hat Asia in Singapore.
(Photo : Gabriel Garcia Marengo)

The NSA ain't got nothin' on the new Snoopy drone Daniel Cuthbert at Sensepost Research Labs and fellow security researcher Glenn Wilkinson created. The two benevolent hackers made Snoopy as part of an experiment that is intended to raise consumer awareness about the inherent vulnerabilities of mobile devices.

Every smartphone and tablet with Wi-Fi onboard automatically searches for new Wi-Fi connections as soon as your preferred Wi-Fi network is out of range. Your smartphone continually searches and searches and searches for Wi-Fi networks that you've joined before until you connect it to one. Cuthbert and Wilkinson set out to show people just how dangerous this constant searching can be for smartphone users. That's why they created the Snoopy drone.

http://www.techtimes.com/articles/4676/20140324/attack-of-the-drones-snoopy-drone-can-steal-your-smartphone-data.htm

What Snoopy does is it captures those beacons and then assists an attacker in mapping out where those SSIDs are located. You can then track a target's geographic movements and history. Snoopy then takes it a step further and actually creates a drone that will spoof one of those networks. As such, when the device connects to that spoofed network, you're in a position to intercept and Man-in-the-Middle the traffic.

If we can do that, we can start finding credentials, stealing cookies for social media accounts, and use it all to expand our influence. Snoopy is really useful in terms of a force multiplier because it automates a lot of these steps.

Another really useful framework for automation is Maltego, by the guys at Paterva. It is a fantastic way to visualize social network connections. When you use it, it's really easy to visualize relationships between data. When you deal with concepts such as social media, they're abstract and are sometimes difficult to comprehend without being able to see a visual representation of them.

Maltego

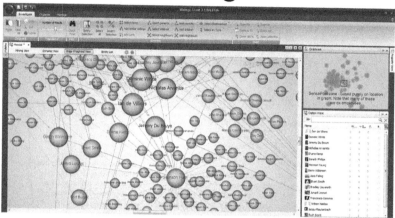

http://maltego.blogspot.com/2011/10/using-socialnet-maltego-to-visualize.html

One of the things you want to do when starting link analysis, is to draw or map a network. For example, if we find John Doe that works for an organization, we want to draw John Doe's social network. If we have Jane Doe too, who is also part of that organization, we want to draw her social network too.

Then we want to start correlating the links between Jane and John, and their networks. Very rapidly, this becomes complex unless we can visually map it all out. What Maltego gives you is a fantastic visualization tool that helps you analyze the relationships between data. The analysis you can do is almost limitless.

You can take an email address and then analyze what social networks it is associated with. You can also look for commonalities and patterns between people. It's really a very powerful tool and there's a lot of value in using a tool like it in this kind of social media reconnaissance and open source intelligence work.

There are numerous tools, a whole multitude of them. I mentioned a tool called The Harvester. It is a Python script that tries to gather this information. There is another tool called Creepy. In truth, there are so many of them and most of them are really useful.

We tend to encourage people to do most of the work manually, at least until they are familiar with what they are doing and understanding this kind of thing, and only migrate to automation when they know what the tool is and how it automates tasks to gather information and perform the analysis. In this manner they can glean the most benefit and value from the tool.

It's pretty clear that social media is a key part of open source intelligence, which is a massive part of reconnaissance-led targeted attacks. What are some lessons to take away from this and how, as an enterprise, can we work toward increasing our security posture on social media?

CHAPTER 6

Conclusion

Here are a couple of lessons to take away:

As a broad concept, the technical aspects of social media are really difficult to block completely, and a number of risks posed by social media are not well understood by most organizations. The standpoint that many take is "well, we'll block access to all these things on our corporate proxy." This is fine, but it's difficult to understand the nuance of this risk, because it doesn't necessarily stop someone using social media from their own device, right?

Hard to Block

http://
www.syslog.com/
~jwilson/pics-i-like/
kurios119.jpg

At many organizations we've worked with, social media networks are blocked on their proxies, but users access them from their own mobile device via the public mobile network. Users are not connecting to the corporate wireless network but they're still on social media. This means the tactic of blocking is difficult. This is because the lines between a personal and professional persona are increasingly becoming blurred.

Blurred Lines

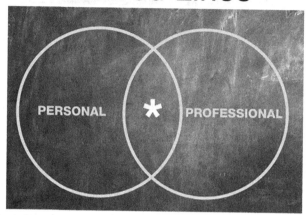

http://blog.hollyhammersmith.com/wp-content/uploads/2013/11/
Braid_PersonalBrand_Overlap1.jpg

Many people have a very big personal presence on social media, but they're also linked with the organization that they work for. They might have a professionally oriented social network on LinkedIn, and they might have information on their professional history, but an attacker may also be able to find personal connections of theirs on their "professional" social network profile.

You might be able to find out where they went to school, their hobbies, and their interests. They might link their professional resource to their personal blog, or their personal Twitter account to a SlideShare account where they host presentations on topics they're interested in. Best of all, these aren't necessarily all professional presentations.

Those lines are really blurring, and it's really difficult to make that distinction anymore in today's day and age. For an organization, it's difficult to just take the approach and say "we're blocking these social networks and we're good to go now." Even if you are doing that, your employees are still out there and your employees are still active on social media.

The key then really starts with growing awareness. People within organizations aren't all malicious and aren't intentionally degrading security. We think in many cases, people don't always understand the mechanisms by which an attacker can use these channels.

They don't always understand the risks, and until you are presented with a profile of yourself and everything you are exposing on social media, it's really difficult to quantify that risk. It's easy to say "Sure people can, but who would want to follow me? I never post anything interesting on social media."

Awareness is key and it's a valuable—an incredibly valuable—tool in being able to say to your employees "An attacker targeting our organization can find out who you are as an employee, and this is what they can find out about you—here's the profile. This is how it is valuable to them." In many cases, once you present the possibilities, and we've seen this happen a few times, they react with, "Wow, I didn't think or know that was possible."

Awareness becomes a very powerful tool, and we don't mean just in terms of security awareness training. We mean in terms of understanding what the risk is to an organization. As an organization, it's really important to understand what your attack surface is. Many enterprises today are performing some form of mapping of their attack surface, and vulnerability analysis on a system level.

You're doing scans from the outside and vulnerability scanning on the inside, and you're potentially running penetration tests. You're hopefully doing some red teaming as well. In the same way you're analyzing your technology profile, you need to also analyze your human attack surface and map it out.

It's really valuable to go through an exercise, or if you don't have the skills in-house to do it yourself, to hire someone to do it for you. Either way, you need to map out your attack surface. Even if you start small and know who your high-risk employees, executives, and other potential targets are, this is a great step forward. Also consider people who work on mergers and acquisitions, and handle secret or sensitive data, investor relations-type people—they are all potential targets.

Attack Surface Mapping

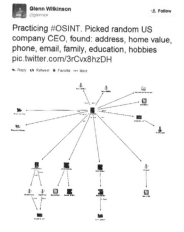

Glenn Wilkinson
@glennzw   Follow

Practicing #OSINT. Picked random US
company CEO, found: address, home value,
phone, email, family, education, hobbies
pic.twitter.com/3rCvx8hzDH

Reply   Retweet   Favorite   ... More

Try to understand what you can find out about that subset of users. Start incredibly small, or start with the CEO of your organization. Go through an exercise of understanding what's exposed on that specific individual and what an attacker could find.

The screenshot we have on the slide is from a Twitter account by Glenn Wilkinson from SensePost. Glenn is one of the lead developers of Snoopy, the tool we mentioned earlier. Glenn and I were teaching a course a few years ago, where one of the components was open source intelligence. As part of his material, Glenn wanted to give an example to our class and he just randomly picked a CEO of a company in the United States. Within a few minutes, he was able to find that individual's:

✓ Address
✓ The value of their home
✓ Their phone numbers
✓ Email addresses
✓ Their family connections
✓ Their education
✓ Their hobbies

That's a really rich profile. The image is just how he mapped this out using Maltego. You can really start to take that information and go a lot deeper from there. You could profile the family members and you could expand from there. It's really scary that there is so much information out there.

While it's very difficult to block the availability of some of this information, it's really important to understand what is available and how it could potentially be used against you so you can prepare and secure the employees concerned.

As an organization, the value starts to become apparent when you are doing regular exercises like spear phishing. At many organizations it is done quarterly and they try to phish their own employees. When you look at those rates, and the rates of success, you understand where to target your remediation. If Jane Doe in accounting is clicking on every spear phishing email and attachment we send her, but she has no profile on the Internet, it's not ideal. However, it's also not very high risk versus a CFO who has a massive public profile and is clicking on every single spear phishing email and attachment.

Maybe we know where to target our education and maybe we need a session specifically with the CFO to educate them on the risks.

Mapping the attack surface is one of your most effective weapons when it comes to awareness.

Printed in the United States
By Bookmasters